NIGHT WEAVERS

Poetic Meditations on Resiliency

MELVIN DOWDY

ARCHWAY
PUBLISHING

Archway Publishing books may be ordered through booksellers or by contacting:

Archway Publishing
1663 Liberty Drive
Bloomington, IN 47403
www.archwaypublishing.com
844-669-3957

ISBN: 978-1-4808-9781-6 (sc)
ISBN: 978-1-4808-9782-3 (e)

Library of Congress Control Number: 2020920286

Print information available on the last page.

Archway Publishing rev. date: 11/18/2020

For Bonnie and all my Night Weavers

Special thanks to my teachers, including Cheryl Pallant,
Katie Ford, and my devoted companion, Bonnie Dowdy.

Contents

Foreword xi
Introduction xv

1 1

While She Slept 3
Trapped 4
Echo of Emptiness 7
Veil of Madness: A Blues Lullaby 9
Sitting Still Until 10
Walking in the Night 11
Old Lovers 12
In the Arms of Rain 14
From Moonlight 15
The Guardians 16

2 17

Dinner with Ann 19
A Sorrow 21
The Eponymous Survivor 24
On Expiration 26
Her Farewell 28

3 29

Fierce Life 31
Anamnesis 33
Barren Stillness at the Refiner's Playground Retreat 34
Did You Notice Forsythia 35
Night Weavers 36
Wood Be Seen: The Congo Mask Exhibit 37

4 . . . . **39**

This Door 41
The Boy with No Ear for Music .43
One Note 46
Silencio 47
This Confusion 48
Swimming 49
In the Stillness of Knowing 50
Black Dancer 51
Trapping the Feral Cat 52

5 . . . . **55**

Easter Reflection 57
Ode to William Stafford 61
Pentecost 63
Beyond Differences: Remembering Amos Oz 65
Rudy Valentine 68
An Uncertain Loneliness 72
Isle of Blue at Kylemore 74

Foreword

Suffering seems to produce three different kinds of people in its wake. The first are those who are broken by it, their life energy and vitality drained from them. They emerge from their time of distress somehow more brittle and cautious, wary of what life will require of them next and doubting their capacity to withstand. Theirs is a *sorrow no flame can burn*. The second type are those who appear to emerge stronger and more determined than ever, confident in their ability to conquer any challenge life throws in their path. Upon closer inspection, however, their courage seems compensatory in nature, an exaggerated response to an unexamined, darker fear that has them in its grip. Theirs is a *'never again'* stance, which life obviously is not obligated to honor. Night Weavers is a collection of poems about a third kind of response to the cauldron of life's challenges and to the quietly extraordinary people who embody it.

As you enter this passage,
know it has a time and season
but no name, no set instructions,
no boundaries, no doctrines.
It only asks one thing —
humility —
which is the bread of vision
for the length of your time
to follow the way.

These are the quietly brave ones who turn and face their dilemma directly. They neither fight nor flee. They may do so knowing this move will cost them everything — their concepts and beliefs, the future they thought was theirs to possess, their faith, their certainty about how life works, even their sense of who they are. They bow, say "Yes" and allow life to have its way with them, perhaps trusting that one day the night weavers will reconcile the twisted and frayed fragments of life into one symphony. They do not wait or need for this to happen. Theirs is a genuine strength, tempered in fire, that neither cowers in the shadows nor announces it greatness from behind a podium. They have come to know who and what they really are. Wild flowers impossibly growing from seams in solid rock. This is enough.

One is reminded of another poet, David Whyte's *Faces at Braga*. The metaphor of a wood carver's artistry is used with this encouragement:

If only our own faces
would allow the invisible carver's hand
to bring the deep grain of love to the surface.
If only we knew
as the carver knew, how the flaws
in the wood led his searching chisel to the very core,
we would smile too
and not need faces immobilized
by fear and the weight of things undone.

Dowdy's work goes deeper, though, revealing a humanity *not painted over grief, but true and gentle...a beauty that does not look to life to shelter.* This earthy, resonant humility, at its core, is tethered to a sacred center from which genuine strength is taken with both a relaxed grip and humble gratitude. The stories shaping these poems are rich and real. A mother denied by police the right to touch her infant, dead now from sudden infant death, until an autopsy can confirm. The mother asks only that her child be baptized. The priest uses her tears for the sacrament. A wife and lover paralyzed by a stroke, the husband afraid to acknowledge to her that he also feels trapped. An aging mother telling her son as she dies, *Promise me you will live well, visit the places where beauty remembers me.* It is this persistent beauty — a beauty *'that will not stay in place'* — that is the distinctive mark Dowdy's collection leaves the reader with.

Night Weavers is a celebration of a *lush, Divine beauty* that lies in the center of our deepest grief, behind our most pressing doubts and penetrating uncertainty. There is a secret inner freedom here that makes sense of our contradictions, calms our agitated minds and binds our wounded hearts. There is essential life bursting open in the center of despair. It is found when we stop looking. This life is not understood intellectually but rather sensed and felt in the heart. Understanding is burned off quickly as dross, with its most-prized concepts and beliefs serving as kindling. Dowdy's poems speak clearly of the unspeakable, and bring light and transcendent joy to those moments that often are beyond the realm of language.

Strangely, I feel honored to be human, honored to be counted among those who have shouldered the burden of sudden disappointment and loss and found a way through. *Will you let the Divine make all your living sacred?* Great poets ask disturbing questions like this and then live their way through to the answer. The only answer that matters is one offered by their body and life, wordless prayers rooted in wonder, a silent beauty felt in presence yet hard to describe, eyes reflecting the fields of God's possibilities.

In Dowdy, we have a man and poet who has allowed his life to *clear the ground where he was standing to make room for a new life, opening himself to a new conversation.* He has the authority only now to encourage us to do the same thing. His brand of resiliency rings true and genuine, forged in the darkest of moments and offered now to us as a guide to say "Yes" to life weaving its way through our hearts to an indescribable wholeness and peace.

Now is the time. Now is your time.

Daniel Holden
Author, *Lost Between Lives — Finding Your Life When the World Goes Dark*
Milwaukee, Wisconsin
September 2020

Introduction

Night Weavers celebrates the beauty and the gravity of being fully human, navigating great sorrows, nourishing the bonds between people, and reconciling one's past with living in the present moment. The poems chronicle a period of major loss and recovery.

Five years ago, my life partner of forty odd years was hospitalized, paralyzed by a spinal cord stroke located at T8 to T11, navel high at her waistline. Every function below her waist was negated in some way. Doubts were grave that she would walk again. We were suddenly on a journey that altered every aspect of our lives and offered few promises of recovery.

I knew what I needed: a practice that would combine mindfulness with daily acceptance of my own experiences, release from assumptions and old habits of the mind, and a daily reclarification of life's meaning and purpose. My writing became the primary source of that practice; I learned to write to stay alive and fully human.

Meditation, as I practice it, aims to quiet the mind until thoughts about life are subdued, allowing a less-filtered perception of life experience. Poems emerge within this way of knowing, often without words; sensations are followed by emotional awareness, shaping tonality, texture, and movement. When I reach this place of seeing my life experience, words, phrases, and images take poetic form. This is what guides and inspires my poetry.

In this collection there are five sections, which illustrate the process of resiliency. The first focuses on paying attention differently in order to notice "what is" and to accept it. Acceptance is the first step toward rediscovering the outcomes of life for which we are willing to endure legitimate suffering. The second focus is discovering what endures, what we retain from our adversity, even in the face of death; all the losses referenced in this section are real-life experiences occurring during the same five-year period. In the third section I shift to a discernment of inner strength and the sources of resiliency we find in others, in our ancestors, and in various forms of spiritual visitation.

What we do, the commitments we make, and the wisdom we claim as our own—this is the shift the fourth section invites you to consider. Resiliency dares to be fully human and to embrace change as a sign of new life. Finally, section 5 expresses my gratitude to those life experiences that have and continue to inspire my life and completes this poetic journey into resiliency.

Resilience is a way of life, not an end to itself. As we learn the art of being with an adversity, we learn the art of being with life in every present moment. I hope these poems will serve as a blessing amid your own adversity.

There's a thread you follow. It goes among things that change. But it doesn't change.

WILLIAM STAFFORD, "THE WAY IT IS"

While She Slept

Alone, downstairs,
bound to bed or wheelchair
after the stroke.
And I, sleeping above,
straining between my quiet
and her labored breathing.
Pain intoned against pain.

Sometimes her sighs
mounted the stairs, lingering,
tearing at my linens.
My desperate walls too weak,
I am thrown into an abyss
where a voice seizes me to confess
the depths of my grief. With what fidelity
could my affection endure our dreadful loss?
Would she disappear within the prison
of this sudden disability?

Dreaming, I heard a reprieve—
a flute singing to the bamboo forest
from which it grew to the lathe
that hewed it, the blade that routed it clear.
The wind rushing through its veins
played a song for mourning. I listened,
and still do.

Trapped

"You feel trapped,"
she said.

Wanting to avoid the obvious,
I answered,

"No I don't!
You know I choose
only what I want,
an exit plan for everything
except you and the boys."

"Stop it," she says.
"Look at me; you're fidgeting.
I know you. This thing, this stroke,
this silent cage has both of us
trapped. Admit it."

Her sincerity never fails;
it bags me, washes over me naked.
I want to be unseen
but cannot hide.

She waits
in a space, holding the question.

I was never ready
for her unlabored honesty,
my insecurity nothing to her,
pretentious, airy fortifications crumbling

before her ordinary words, reminding me
how long she intended to wait.

"Okay, I admit feeling trapped.
There it is."

She says nothing, waiting for me to say more.

"Be hurt, don't be hurt!
Whatever! This thing, this stroke,
depleted the oxygen; something is dying
inside me, and all I do is wait
for whatever another round of rehab promises."

"You sound pissed off," she said,
"at me, the stroke, the fall, my broken hip,
the second fall that broke my wrist,
the biologics, the dimmed sexuality."

Slumping in my chair, raising
my eyes to hers,

"No, not really, but yes, often.
And sometimes I wonder if
you can see me, how I am nothing
under the weight of your ubiquitous voice.
Even unspoken, you come to me,
pressing into me until I recognize myself
more clearly.

"You do not understand.
I cannot escape you. Believe me,
I have tried and spied
upon other loves, so many shadows

that thrust me into this choice
to bind my life to you,

to this brood chamber, where
you and I have formed
something called We, and there
who can refuse this death?"

Nothing left unsaid,
we finish breakfast, and I wash the dishes.

Echo of Emptiness

The dark basement
holds ten thousand things, forgotten

boxes stacked full upon shelves,
some marked correctly, some sagging, a shoebox
leaning on another with a scribbled note attached,
"Goodwill."

Someday this damp cellar will be vacated
by complaining relatives speculating

why this, why that, how come
something that old might have been stored,
what the hard drive contains, wondering,
Where are the bowls to match these tops?

Someday these painted walls will try to resist
the moisture of an underground vault.

Wires and pipes like wild roots dangling,
the clogged drain, the back door jammed
holding in dust; broken glass, the sticky paper traps
for invading crickets and mice.

On that final day, this chamber will hold no life,
no unopened packages, no ripped pages or photographs,

no tattered memories of foreign tours,
no journals of choices and failures,
no unhinged doors set beside the walker,
no wheelchair or a bedside commode.

Only stains will remain from old paint cans,
rusty tools, a leaky pipe, scraps of an old bed frame,

stuffing from a sagging mattress,
the shadow marks of a rummage sale headboard
next to the rusty rectangular etches where
crates of old sliver trays were stored.

Listen—your discerning heart may hear an echo
accompanied by trumpets, guitars, and a maraca

keeping tempo, while ghosts like swirling dervishes
transform the emptiness into a dance saloon
recalling desperate, wild nights of love.

Veil of Madness: A Blues Lullaby

The air hangs thick with nothing to say
When my mind breaks into a blues lullaby.
Shuffle along, the hardwood floor singing,
"There ain't no reason to cry."

Each step a phrase, each breath a rest,
Grooving a lyrical solitude,
Leaving a space, madness a place
Soothed only by the moon.

Sleepy time covers my desperation.
Turn down my bedsheets, I'm almost gone,
Dreaming of you in days of our youth,
The veil of madness drawn.

Sitting Still Until

The morning calls
  you to rise, be present
    as the cardinal chatters,
      stretching his velvet coat.

The to-do things line up
  like children waiting for the bus,
    each task due, some overdue,
      you mean to get them done.

No hurry, it's early, there's time
  to get ready, wash, shave, dress
    for work, tie the laces of your shoes
      in a double knot carefully.

Approach the door, wake her
  with kisses, asking which cereal she prefers,
    set the table, slice the fruit, heat the tea,
      talk about the day.

"Not much," she replies.
  She will circle the block on her scooter,
    check the computer, catch up on a few things
      overdue; who knows what they mean.

Pausing, your eyes glean the truth
  of what matters, who we are,
    one morning kiss to carry your presence.
      The squirrel chases another up the crape myrtle.

Walking in the Night

In steady tempo, robed in light,
Two stars walk across the night,
Conversing to keep abreast
Of daily news, points of view,
As friends bound by secrets do.

What have you heard? Better yet,
How do you know to make sense of it,
Some sliver of joy worth repeating?

A song on my mind stuck all day.
Our children for hours at play.
How fine to go dancing.
You could wear the pearls I fancy
And I, in a tux with red bow tie,
Remembering rhythms we learned—
Our steps, cortes, swivels, and turns.

Dawn approaches, almost home.
Tomorrow comes sunlit alone when
Hidden in light I cannot find you.
Wait for me in the stars' delight,
Guiding our steps to midsummer's night.

Old Lovers

Circling the lake,
Two of us talking for hours
Of life's endeavors,
Passionate moments,
Sifting insights about the absurd
Lingering questions. One makes a suggestion,
The other proposes an alternative.
It was easy to drift and stumble
Where the sidewalk lifted.
The roots of dogwoods lined the shore.

Once I was boasting,
As I often did,
How I came to this lake,
Recommending to my date
We watch the fountain changing
From blue to red, silver to orange,
Lifted in the air, suggesting
Summer rain, a great place
For young lovers.

My companion laughed, chiding
How I'd failed to mention this tidbit,
Leading her to believe she was the first.
Quickly recovering, I assured her
She was forever the last.

Then we sat to watch the bare dogwoods
Through moonlight, and to listen
To the cold of winter, holding tightly

Dreams of growing old together,
Like the geese who fly home to this place.

We are certain only of a few things.
We are immersed in wonder,
Embedded in the promises we made,
Celebrating our accidental abundance.
With courage we walk a little way,
Fold her walker into the car,
And drive home.

In the Arms of Rain

Under steady hands
rain came yesterday,
snuffing out twilight
into dark thunder
gentle enough to hear
geese calling each other
to fly home.

Under steady hands
earth lay subdued
in tranquil response
as rain's long fingers
penetrated earth's soft muscle,
kneading, rhythmically receding,
lingering lightly, withdrawing,
rushing to fill the empty spaces.

Under steady hands
covering everything,
speaking a blanket of memories,
earth recalls
how cherished it is
to fall asleep
completely immersed
in the arms of rain.

From Moonlight

I am moon to your light
Over the deep waters
Night into night, moving the tides
Always closer to shore.

My dark heart waits to hear
The sound of your voice
Over the rippling waters—
Lapping, laughing, disturbing.

My forgetfulness, recognizing now
What good or evil I have done
For strangers, for friends, for lovers
Known and discovered, finding

Courage and unconstrained passion
Illuminating this formless, patient
Conversation, where I see again
Your luminous face.

The Guardians

The twin oaks guard entry to our house,
arms raised for good seasons, bowed
when tossed by storms, bent over in grief
and sometimes broken; they stand steady
in winter's brittle gray, waiting for the days
to grow longer again.

Like them, time rooted us in beauty
lit by the sun; while in the dark times,
we stretched to touch the depth within,
which taught our fidelity to thrive, to form
a space in-between, a canopy of welcome
and shade for summer breezes.

Tree nymphs living in the branches
aim to preserve, though they know trimmers
quick to the blade. Wise enough for watchful waiting,
wondering which falls first, and which one remains
a solitary witness to arbor guests. Alas,
time insists only one will bide.

Each year hurricanes come, discouraging forecasts
break old records, sea levels continue to rise.

This cottage near the Carillon is strong enough
to keep us dry from the rains. The guardians shield us
through the seasons of heat and give sweet sleep
as we live our place in time.

... like an iceberg between the shoulder blades.

MARY OLIVER, "WHEN DEATH COMES"

Dinner with Ann

At dinner tonight—
Irish stew mixed with friendship—
four of us spoke to depths
where time ends; we needed
to lift up our common journey home.

     With grace you spoke of a year, maybe two
living well,

Being a presence to grandchildren.
Death to ALS, your final gift—a whole life
condensed into living intentionally, sipping
precious moments, not rushing to the end,
not pushing for joy, just letting be—
hoping you will not sink into despair
but take courage to stay alive in a body
that is failing you; your mind clear,
witnessing your life, watching yourself
becoming more physically disabled.

     And we could see you almost taking flight,
more spiritually able.

We cannot tell, not one of us,
how soon our own death will appear.
Just the same, the archway is there
in the distance; some of us can see the exit sign.
We do not know how to calculate or cherish
fewer days given to live the mission of our lives.
What we do know is this,

We must be serious now. We must play
in the field of God's possibilities.

When I encounter someone
like you entering death's corridor,
I am drawn closer, grasped by a sacred,
unqualified patience, life's mystic desperation
seeking joy, often extended to fascination, a touch
of terror passing through the veil; reaching
with them, I want to reach through them.

Keep me in mind when you need me,
I will come to you.

I will find my makeup and the silly hat,
the oversized shoes, a dress shirt
with big black buttons, pure white gloves,
a cane to help this clown––lost in prayer––wobble
into your room.

My smile, not one painted
over my grief, but true and gentle.

My hand in your hand, your spirit guide
if you need me to be; for Ann,
I need you, we all need you, drawing near
as we make this journey into light.

A Sorrow

There is a quiet reverence
bordering fear, a fog of despair
in every corner clinging to the room.
The ER nurse points out the stall,
pulls back the curtain and says,
"This is the chaplain," then leaves us
in that silence.

  I don't know what to do, what to say.

Standing a few feet from the stretcher,
shoulders hunched over, arms crossed in front,
the mother is sobbing, the uniformed officer
opposite her. Each watching near disbelief
a perfect three-month-old infant
swaddled, a coral-white likeness
of death on display.

"They won't let me hold my baby,"
she pleads. Her eyes pressing urgent upon me,
glancing to the table and then back to me.
Then to where her beloved is motionless,
who she had held, cradled, and nursed this morning.
Now nothing but comfortless innocence,
her first and only child.

  Lost in loss, no words, senseless, absurd …

When crib death steals a child,
the so-called civil requirements of law
are a simple and brutal certainty.

The officer's explanation sticking
like bones in the throat, he wanted to
but couldn't allow touch, not before
forensics came for their examination.

Holy Mary, Mother of God, pray for us …

She petitions for one favor.
Within her narrative of a sunny room
she painted, the lace curtains, the first toys,
the baptism delayed, she asks now
a simple grace, considered vital to her peace
of mind, she cannot rest unless her child can rest,
"Would you bless my baby girl?"

To Thee do we cry, poor banished children of Eve …

Nodding consent, the officer steps back,
enough room given me to come closer
to form in the midst of her terror a safer space,
our private chapel lit within a hidden baptistry,
a Cross hung on a nearby wall portraying the risen Christ
whose arms stretch to gesture "Welcome Home,"
in a hospital commissioned and named Bon Secours.

A resonance binds us, abandoning
all thought, penetrated by a luminous mystery
guiding us through the clef, and into
synchronous, pneumatic life. Like rushing waters
we are confirmed in the transcendent Christ
beyond the gravity of all law, in whose arms
he gathers his lambs.

That we may be made worthy …

My hands trembling, I raise a thumb
to collect the embrocation of her wet eyes.
I pass from her body to her child a condensation,
anointing her child's forehead where
the sign of the cross now joins them,

"In Nomine Patris, et Filii, et Spiritus Sancti."

Then a sorrow no flame can burn.

The Eponymous Survivor

The forgotten summer burns across
her graveyard mound. Her footstone
displaced, moved to the side where
gravediggers left it after drinking a pint,
maybe two. They must have talked about her,
why her grave was laid between two men.

Brothers, veterans from the war; they noted
she married both, one dying in forty-four,
while still newlywed. The other brother returned,
found his brother's widow, picked up her life,
what was left for him to salvage. Imagine
the grief filling that house, the two bereft,
straining love through a sieve of mourning.

Imagine the love letters that stopped after
men in uniform drove the lane, August of forty-four,
to hand this girl from Fisher's Farm the final note of regret––
Gravediggers know things, picturing her reading those
letters over and again, the President's regret, while
she sat on the big front porch, the back steps, or walking
to Fisher's Store near the tracks at Elko station,
where locals meet to argue over politics, debate
crop rotation or prices at the farmer's market.

They notice the footstone, a Purple Heart inscribed
for the younger. Gravediggers hear secret things,
the lonely dead talk of children born, of hidden rage,
and trips made to recover from old wounds, how
the furtive fire of love consumes the bitterness
of grief, leaving just a trace of fidelity.

Who––the gravediggers ask––will remember these three,
and where are the letters, who will read them, collect
the black and gray photographs? Who will brush the dust
settling upon raw heroism? Who will unravel
the compacted sacrifices; who will learn from them,
their patient embolization of the heart, comprehend
how they dislodged the piercing woundedness,
and scattered compassion over undaunted life? And
who was she, that for eleven years prevailed as bondswoman
for two brothers, their eponymous survivor?

On Expiration

One week later, life hasn't changed.
I miss her, true, but I am contented with
her good death, living so well,
learning how to be happy,
being grateful, generous, and engaged,
difficult or not, often trying hard
to avoid the appearance of ignorance,
seeming uneducated, which she hated.
An uncultured country girl, she was gifted
at putting on appearances, hiding imperfections,
few compared to her natural beauty and charm
emanating from an endless depth of compassion,
a sentimentality fresh as gardenia.

Lady poverty taught her to worry,
a habit of stuffing closets full of things
she or someone else might need someday.
Saving gift-wrapped boxes of new clothes,
Ribbons, and cards to remind her of who gave them.
Coats, hats, scarves, gloves for every season—
if she could remember she had them.
Never waste food; always taste it
to see if something has passed its expiration,
which may have been what made her sick,
throwing up for days just before the heart attack.
Too much stress on that ninety-five-year-old body
sent her to the ICU to say farewell
before crossing the bridge home.

I'm contemplating a summer
devoted to Mother's memory, learning
to be happy again, living fully engaged,
discovering gratitude, becoming more generous—
at least with some folks; screw the others.
I'll try hard to get this old boy back in shape,
if not for appearances' sake then to check my redneck habits,
not pretending to hide my imperfections,
not waiting to begin again, but daring to live
without her blessings and embellished praise.
Take time to clean out closets, pack up boxes
of worn-out shoes, faded shirts, wide paisley ties,
mismatched socks, and always remember—
throw out anything with an overdue expiration.

Her Farewell

Unhindered by time,
forming palm and long fingers into a single gesture,
her hand approaches his face.

With distilled gentleness
she places her thumb perfectly
in the curvature between his cheek and nose,
forefingers extending to his ear, her ring finger
and smaller one rest around his jaw,
she cultivates their affection.

Lying with her upon a cushion
in the dim light, layered by flickering candles,
the room filled with intensity, like orchids
opening for farewell, inhaling the final scent
of tender vulnerability, he watches her lips move––
she is dancing with infinity.

"Promise me you will live well,
visit the places where beauty remembers me,
listen to the music and the laughter,
talk with strangers like they were your best friend,
drink wine in the afterglow of sunsets,
know that I am forever near."

She leans closer to say,
"You will remember me."

We are the fierce stretching for the light.

MELVIN DOWDY

Fierce Life

I first realized I was lost
the day the bully tore the dog tag
from my neck, the one I wore
for my fallen father,
whose name I bore,
a hero's insignia.

But I was not mean enough, strong, brave
or daring enough to fight him—
less like my father than I wished—
and that injury lingered like an equation
of unknown value. What name is mine?

For life lived, unlived, the best of it passing,
the worst coming, like a bully stealing someone
in search of a name.

Those old haunting threats return
in dreams of failures, regretful meanderings,
still searching to know the truth of himself,
the choices made, the passing faces
of those loved. With the birth of fatherhood,

the slow melding of wisdom begins a new habit
of the heart, knowing the courage necessary
to be truly with another in their uncertainty,
in their rage, in their longing to know,
in their searching for a name.

I am in this present moment the priest
who was the keeper of swords, who laid them aside

for a clay chalice made of dust collected from an army
of dead heroes who fought for peace.

I am their memory of what matters most,
what is worthy of life, what cannot be taken
nor borrowed, only lived.

You may ask who am I? Go then
to the wall of names found in graveyards
and memorial parks; search for my name there,
and know I am etched in the cold stone,
engraved onto the walls of sacrifice,
mingled among the grains of sand,
the fading image you try to read
on old gravestones.

Do not hold me in your thoughts.
Hold instead all the children of all the wars,
especially those you are about to wage.
Place around their necks the name
that tells them how precious they are
and the fierce life they must live
in search of a name.

Anamnesis

Your voice sometimes recalls for me the bow,
a woody cello, perhaps echoes of a slide trombone
or some resonant chanting other.

Time swings with a pulsing unseen pendulum
of hours, of days, of months passing into
the last trace of you beside the river.

We lie there, fireflies lighting the night,
velvet darkness folding into silence,
rejoined in the anamnesis of brotherhood.

Barren Stillness at the Refiner's Playground Retreat

Beside the frozen lake in this time of icy stillness,
the barren tree ponders the deep currents
quietly raging below, clearing the decaying waste,
preparing new life to spawn in the warmth
of hidden springs. This towering witness stands
with its branches twisted by paths taken
through summer shadows, the long desolate nights
it endured while stretching toward the light,
willing to bend, to navigate any disturbance, always rising.

A bluish mist cloaks its hollows this snow-melting
morning. A stillness hovers within its branches
asking what sound earth's astonishing beauty makes
except to assure us we are safe in her embrace
as we kneel in ice and snow below this ageless witness,
receiving nature's strength with unspeakable gratitude.

Like the tree before this barren stillness, we are the constant,
stretching for the light; we are the witnesses, we are
the process daring to raise our hands in this strange
classroom, our eyes filled with tears, our hearts
in our throats. We rise to ask a question, uncertain
what question to ask but demanding an answer. We know
the teaching has begun. Trusting that our inquiry
be compassionate, we will unfold more connected,
and our answer will be playful, though surely it will be fierce.

Did You Notice Forsythia

Did you see her walking—supple, swaying, tall, and lean—
among Yoshino cherries, azalea admiring her
as she runs along the footpath beside the lake
in springtime's labor, birthing, vibrant, lusty?
From the garden she welcomes morning, conducting
a stanza of the "Halleluiah Chorus" along the freeway.
Hiding behind the house she plays wedding games
with a flush of green lilies and Lenten roses.
Did you hear the standing ovation echoing
from city balconies to the Appalachian roadside,
nature's magnificent community bursting with appreciation?
Life refuses to shelter; beauty will not stay in place.

Night Weavers

I have seen them carrying skeins,
hanks of blue and orange, tenuous ghosts
like night clouds making silent rounds of grief.

They know our labor, mistakes we chose
to forget, unfinished lives we tried to repair,
the failed certainties buried in memory.

They witness everything, the invisible motion
threading the loom, the genesis rhythm
rocking as lovers do in slow, timeless welding.

Why do they come faithfully to us?
What joy or terror do they seek from
the remnants we might wish to discard?

When night weavers visit, their ancestral craft
examines the twisted yarn, delicately lifting and
tucking frayed, unruly edges, the weight of seams.

No matter how tender their vigil, they reweave
to full-length things hidden until weft and warp,
a new pattern is made pure as the moon's reflection.

Wood Be Seen:
The Congo Mask Exhibit

Fierceness here
in this place,
deep wells of knowing
and not knowing.

Ancestral spirits brought together
a tribal gathering of
timeless eyes; the universe
rotating, a convergence
of ancient roots.

Here it is impossible to hide.
A blanket of watchful eyes
has thrown upon our bowed minds
a fire that consumes all modern pretenses.

These swirling masks scream,
"Honor me." The wood whispers,
"See me." A stale harmonizing breath,
frost from the lungs of earth's center,
fills the air, dizzying, entrancing us
to dance, painted with the white face of death.

Nature scraped crimson red
from Baobab bark, berries, and grasses
blended azure blue, then painted human flesh
with brushstrokes of time and magic. From chin
to forehead, across pale cheeks are seen spotted
cruel diseases, a potent zest for life,

a defiant invitation to anyone who dares to survive
this harsh, pandemic swamp of life.

Untamable forces are aligning, drumming
an army of witnesses, stomping, shaking,
rummaging, raking, swirling, slapping, clapping,
tipping, stepping in motion till every creature's
skin-of-the-world is stepping out with feathers of fire,
terror harmonized with joy, in ritual observance
of life dancing with death, under penalty of drums,
in rhythms drawn from human endurance.

If you don't break your ropes while you're alive,
do you think
ghosts will do it after?

———

KABIR, "THE TIME BEFORE DEATH"

This Door

Isn't this the way life goes,
this corridor of doors?
Most were opened, some passed
even after glances within,
worn bare, the paint chipped away,
door handles that no longer shine.
This one or that one may never shut tightly.

You reach the one that has been sealed,
where a sign reads, "Repairs Needed!"
Your first task is to dismantle the lock,
slip off the stiff handle that's nearly frozen in place
by years of rigid answers, lessons refused.
Keeping it shut felt safer back then.
Now it is time.

The bolt is slightly jammed, fixed
into the strike plate
from repetitious protests,
each one your chance
to bet on life extended, red or black,
conservative or liberal, straight or gay—
there must be a correct way—keep trying.

Now the seal must be broken.
Rimmed from top to bottom,
you must slip the blade into the crusted crack,
slowly but forcefully, willfully, not avoiding
the agglutinant of age. Each time the blade releases
the door, you hear it pop, loosened,

until the whole construction of your neglect
breaks free, shakes a little, startled.

The hinges, too, are tight,
but they firmly grasp the frame,
constant over the years for upon its strength
the axis of life can move again.
The door swings open upon arms
that moved stones from tombs.
This time you are passing through,
leaving your old self behind.

The Boy with No Ear for Music

My mother,
when she insisted, made
water flow upstream,
dawn break two hours early,
grown men suffer weak knees
under the weight of her argument.

So it was
on that first day of school,
she convinced the band director
her son wanted to play the horn,
not the drums, against his bitter refutation
that drumming required no ear.

The boy, he said,
    was not musically talented.

The horn would likely yield
an alien sound. Better judgment
to stick to simplistic rhythms,
fewer embarrassments.

He, the band director,
    lost the argument.

Trumpet purchased, lessons arranged, woven between
weekly instruction, daily practice, fourth-period band,
the boy sat in the last chair, last section,
at the end of a row. There he was
in the corner, almost hidden from view,

a deafferent segmentation,
reducing sounds from the bell of the horn, small farts
spurting from pistons clumsily depressed
by the boy with no ear for music.

Upstairs, above the music store,
    lessons progressed.

First, unencumbered breathing, correct posture necessary
allowing a single, focused stream of air
penetrating the mouthpiece, producing a buzzing sound
held gently in-hand, not yet in the lead tube of the horn.

Once perfecting the sound
from the detached mouthpiece,
billows of laughter could be heard on the streets below
as this boy who slipped the mouthpiece into the horn
to form a clear midrange G, neither flat nor sharp,
a sustained column of harmonic purity.

Gradually, single notes
became scales adeptly performed,
from whole to quarter notes played evenly,
round sounds pianissimo, fortissimo, staccato, tenuto
without brassy colors, a mellow melodic tonality.
Even naive ears could hear a music of distinctive clarity.

Each June parents came
    to a concert intended to display

a year's achievement,
from marches and fight songs, redacted arrangements
by well-known composers, to hymns,
occasional solos, featured quartets.

That year—and every year following—
Mother won her argument,
pointing to the kid in the first chair, first section,
solo or duet, that round, full sound like a signature,
a lingering vibration, a genial wave upon which
the mind could float, until gently disappearing in thin air—

By the boy
    with no ear for music.

One Note

One note sustained, clarity dissolving
Into space, searching the universe
For home, played between the melodies,
Chords and discords in high and low registry,
One among their melancholy, one note of hope

Within the destiny of beauty, her shape
The light of one star, a single breath.
Or a sigh floating on the breeze among
Trees of the rain forest, golden
As a blade of sunlight resting upon

The rim of a flower, as heavy as a drop
Of rain penetrating the mirror lake,
Welcomed by all into the fellowship
Of creation—true to itself,
one note.

Silencio

"Silencio" is placed on her lapel with
instructions to speak to no one, nor
be spoken to, yet seen by inquiring eyes
testing her resolve, her unqualified entrance
into this discerning fellowship.

Retreat houses are serious places
designed to throw seekers headlong
into a densely populated wilderness
of their agitated minds, desperate
to come hungry to their senses.

What is this affliction? To deny physical comforts,
cramped into a cell, a prisoner of rooms
where doors stay open, the floors creak under
the strange footsteps of whoever brought her here.

Hours pass into days of slowly unfolding time,
an evolving rhythm threads an inner freedom,
disorder displaced, shambles collected and sorted
into the corners of wordless prayers until someone
is making peace with all her contradictions.

> Speak to me lush, divine beauty!
> I am prepared for a new conversation. I know
> You are waiting for me within all things
> in the long night, in the first light splashed
> upon the hibiscus outside my window.

Late in the day, just before dusk settles,
she hears the whispering of trees; she sees
blue oceans rushing through their limbs.
Her senses cleansed, her mind becomes silent.

This Confusion

This moment of confusion is nothing but
    your own brain chatter construction—

intentions that didn't matter, the fast
    or slow pace sounding off.

Below the balcony, on noisy streets, faint traces
    of meanings you call your life—

flinging you into activity, rushing to do
    but reluctant to undo the painful maintenance

of what you say is necessary if only in the service of
    your vague "so-what" destiny.

Settle down, stretch your mind to the hidden within,
    a silent art forming nonmaterial reality, the shape of

life not seeking but sourcing hidden, kindred spirits
    who come from millennium, who mark your soul,

who align their life-giving spirals to shape
    every motion into an arc, stretching, reaching

where the tiniest measure of your will is set free,
    becoming an undetermined, unimpaired alchemy,

the beauty of life, hope thrusting into the future,
    attending your unfolding, unknowing imagination.

Swimming

If you don't swim in the waters
and don't dance in slow motion
to see what your body can do floating
slowly, suspended light upon its surface,

you may not catch the rainbows
or bathe in her colors.
Life's possibilities, lost and replaced,
will constantly fail to delight you.

We all come from the sea,
who whispers to us in our sleep.
But dreams are only dreams
until we wake up to who we are.

It is time to dive into your joy
and shake off the blah, blah, blah
of discouraging voices you carry around
in your head. Trust me, they lie.

In the Stillness of Knowing

In the stillness of knowing the edge,
his mind strains not to blur but to clear the blind spots,
afford flashes of insight upon the dark impulses
he must learn to face, his passions no longer covered up by lies.
He is facing the truth about himself, a middle-aged man
whose numb body was lately awake.

Head buried, rocking back, opening his eyes
that glisten with years of desperate waiting,
a question he had avoided, feared, dismissed,
and forgotten until today—he knows,
like fire not smothered by stone, and before
whatever gods might be listening,
this is the hour to write the suicide note.

He could just walk out the door, leave
the pretty little house where the debts
were made, paid, remade, saved, receipts
to prove what life means, or buy another hour of dreams
and be sure to tell yourself all is well, carefully
put fresh flowers in the vase, hang the paintings,
in their museum-quality frames, looking onto an Italian landscape.

Today is the perfect day, he thought,
to wipe the canvas clean; a cruel but true
variation of death, this quiet hour.

Sighing, he reaches for the long leather strap,
rises to his feet, makes certain his grasp is firm,
double-knots his old shoes, and then leaves the house
to walk the dog.

Black Dancer

Wild and reckless,
tapping, turning, a daring
takeoff beyond the music, beyond the form
seduced by body's heat; hands, arms,
feet refusing to retreat, knowing
only a desire to soar

through rivers of air
moving round, pulsing within,
rhythms making dark olive skin glisten
in, out of, flashing light visible
then invisible again, leaping,
gravity losing its hold

on a Black dancer captured, formed
only by freedom surging
with strength, implausible line, a burning heart
summoned, a flourishing spirit with face,
eyes, breath lifted, returning beauty
to irresistible grace, the turbulent defiance of being.

Trapping the Feral Cat

The trap is set, waiting for the feral cat.
A morsel of food carefully placed, a taste
of chicken and fish in a little round tin
clinking against the metal cage, echoing
like keys rattling against a lock
to seal its hopeless fate—this predator
who feasts on mourning doves and finches.

Excitement seizes me, imagining
his curious approach, cautious, hungry
calculations, surveying the shiny unfamiliar
contraption; his paws worn tough by city streets
pressing suspect upon the metal grate. Black-yellow eyes
glance through four square crisscross patterns; he sees
a world soon to be out of reach—his world

of dominion, to go where he wished,
to sleep in shelter or in rain, fed by strangers,
preying upon the wild birds and the small rodents, then
climbing on a backyard shed to survey his frontier.
Free and wild, in full possession of his daring life,
the dangerous stealth rounding, supple prowler
keen to capture and never be caught.

Tomorrow I will check again to see
if he's there. I'm hoping that this contest is over,
knowing my sorrow will blur my vision of him.
I will grieve my deep feral connection, my bond
to his wild, untamed majesty, his solitary simplicity.

Trapped, I carried him in the cage to my car,
drove twenty miles outside of town, passing rivers
and interstate highways until reaching the countryside.
I placed the cage on an old logging trail, lifted the gate,
and stood still as I watched him escape. Free.

There will soon be no more priests. Their work is done ... Every man shall be his own priest.

WALT WHITMAN, "LEAVES OF GRASS"

Easter Reflection

Where was Thomas?
Where was the twin, Didymus?
The disciples we know
were huddled in fear behind locked doors,
hiding from arrest and being strung up like Jesus.
Following him would exact a price!
They were fugitives without the One who had calmed
even the disturbances of the sea.

Surely a second fear
held them locked behind the shutters
in the dim light where shadows seem to be
larger than life.
Mary had news of an empty tomb,
and she told of meeting the risen Lord.
Incredulous! Could it be? Had he risen? What to believe?

Fear can torment hope,
turn hearts to stone, take the light out of our eyes,
leaving one blind with anticipation,
endlessly watching our deepest desires
shrinking under the weight of our disappointment
locked in a room
of not-knowing despair!

There they were,
sometimes weeping, whispering in low tones,
grieving hearts that cannot help speculate
against a backdrop of conspiracy
the future—if there is one—

as they peek through cracks around the door,
collectively holding their breath
when unfamiliar sounds make their hearts beat too loudly,
asking, "Will life ever be the same?"

Again I ask you, "Where was Thomas?"
Roaming the streets? Hiding
in the alleyways,
choosing to be alone?
Or was he left behind in the mayhem, forgotten?
Was he missing or had the Holy Communion
that once made them whole
now shrunk into self-concern,
broken and finished?

When Thomas finally found his friends,
they were waiting for him with news
he could not believe.
Something had changed, but not in him.
He would not believe their terrifying, surreal story.

How could it be?
In the very place where he now stood
Jesus had stood,
greeting them in peace, breathing on them
the Holy Spirit?
Had he missed the assurance of all he hoped for?

"No, I cannot listen! There were too many questions!
Nonsense!
Show me! Show me! Show me!
Or else shut up, and leave me the hell alone!"

We know how
the story of Thomas ends
like ours, a thousand times, yesterday, tomorrow.
No mystery is needed to explain our unbelief
perpetually unaware,
unable to accept someone else's word
for what seems impossible.

Resurrection is no good news,
only an absurd humiliation for those searching alone
in the streets for a way home.
Nothing seems able to replace being alone
in the belief
that God is dead.

Slowly, the dark eyes of unbelief
are blessed by Someone
who gives an invitation to come closer,
to see and believe for oneself,
to understand the impossibility of grace.
Doubt has not prepared our hearts to believe
that all life has been redeemed,
every struggle graced so that
human consciousness can see the risen Christ.

Divine revelation moves us
from unbelief to believing,
from solitude to communion.
When we encounter the beloved friend,
we see the wounds that tear
the scars of ruthless beatings.
We see the evidence
that human suffering will be redeemed, in every form
reclaimed.

For Spirit-God
so loved the world that
giving, pouring out one's life, emptying one's self
have become the pulse of universal law,
making all things sacred
and breathing life into dead bodies
like yours and mine
so that we may cast shadows that heal,
becoming human against all odds!

Is now the time
to listen to your fear of believing,
to accept the solitude that surrounds your questions,
let your fears be blessed
for as long as is needed to make you holy?
When Jesus comes with his invitation
to move into a new house,
a house of believing,
a house of communion with those chosen
to bear everything human,
will you let the divine make all your living sacred?

Ode to William Stafford

Unexpected, it finds
you
standing in the temple
of your disbelief,
bowed down upon
your knees under
a pandemic threat.

Maybe it was on Facebook
someone dared
admit feeling terrified
when you realized
something at our core
draws us together.

Social distance—strange,
that new attention
to the fabric of connection—
a depolarization,
wiping down
all differences except
our vulnerability.

It forces us home to the alpha,
the hour of beginnings,
seeing the birth face, we smile
as from the womb.

You start sending emails
to friends, past roommates,
urging fresh vision, pouring

kindness, and appreciation
over the gift of others.
Tuesday's child again, to reimagine
the web of our belonging.

Pentecost

Within you, well below
the street noise filling your head,
lies the center,
an open chamber where
your breath refines and unbinds
all desire, every fear, leaving no trace
of old pretenses.

Sit, rest, receive
the one who has pondered
your return, who knows the path
persistent, its preparation, who can teach you
the solitude you contemplated but didn't allow
until now.

Feel the wind within,
stay with its voice
like thunder.
Its lips sip the fire, the wine
of this awakening hour
when tombs are opened,
and you see the ground where you were standing
cleared to make room for your new life.

As you enter this passage,
know that it has a time and season
but no name, no set instructions,
no boundaries, no doctrines.
It only asks one thing—

humility,
which is the bread of vision
for the length of your time
to follow the way.

Beyond Differences:
Remembering Amos Oz

What does it mean?
I must ask of anyone with a solution,
what does it mean
when someone hidden from sight,
from some nearby advantage
takes a shot at you,
when bullets are flying
beyond denial,
aimed at your naive head,
asking if this is happening, could this be real?
Before you know it,
you've gone and bought a gun because
in this zone of terror, you don't know,
you cannot calculate
the where or when or who.
You are ready.
You're not going to just lie down.
You're not going to be a victim
lined up for slaughter
like a million Jews to die in gas chambers,
or villages of men, women, and children
standing beside the ditches
as they wait and watch,
the earth filing up with death,
and some just wounded, buried alive.

No, not this time!
The day arrives. You aim

to kill him, the one you now carry
in your blood as enemy.
The bullets are flying
off your tongue
in the endless repetition
of hatred and blame,
up to the last bullet of stinging rage
flying out from your soul,
beyond your body, beyond restraint,
beyond reason. You ride on the wings
of its naked flight.
You can hear the hissing sound of the wind
on either side; you see the light split by speed,
amazed by the sheer velocity
of hatred. Nearer and clearer,
you can see him, the eyes of your enemy
startled wide when your condemnation reaches
the first layer of hatred,
his reasoning cracked open.
He is screaming, and you are screaming back.

What does it, what could it mean?
What can be recovered? What will not decay
beyond your body, beyond your will,
beyond calling anyone to restore order and justice
beyond the hope for brotherhood
as life goes on in this pledged fight for human dignity?

Where beyond the edge of empty promises
can dreams of peace take root?
Where can we imagine
the demarcation of a more fertile ground,
not soaked with the blood of hatreds,
where the depth of our collective committed moral vision

is bound by the practice of peace,
beyond self-interest or shallow graves,
where the small and fragile seeds of hope
can grow, can unmask a solution
beyond differences?

Rudy Valentine

Our church janitor,
a Black man
whose floors shined
as devotion to his faith,
as the pews glistened
under the horseshoe-arched windows,
the sun
poured in rainbows,
dancing
in the sanctuary.

After Sunday school
I'd find him
in the basement,
sitting in a chair,
Bible open to
a favored passage.
The brooms, a buffer,
and the furnace pipes
made a quiet hermitage.

Rudy didn't come
to church ever,
always assuring me
he was praying
his own prayers,
talking to Jesus,
an in-person conversation
flowing.
And sometimes,

he let me listen.
And when he sang,
there was a holiness about him.

I confess
he made me feel holy,
which made his staying
in the basement
make no sense.
My parents explained
he was Black,
meaning he had his way, and
we White folks
had ours—
whatever that meant.

Weekdays
I'd bike to the church,
find Rudy
busy buffing hallways,
singing some old hymn
about somewhere.
One time he showed me
the trick
for controlling the buffer,
sweeping right to left,
finding a balance necessary
to avoid
slamming into a wall.

When the preacher left
for visits,
we'd go to the sanctuary
like kids sneaking into a show,

lift the keyboard lid,
sit side by side
while he played jazz tunes
from his old days
performing in Harlem
and in Village clubs
all night,
the wood knocking against the keys.

Years later,
his wife died.
I went to his home,
tapped on the screen door.
A huge German Shepherd greeted me,
intimidating,
while Rudy shouting
from the back room,
telling me
he was coming quickly
then finding me sitting on the floor,
his dog lying beside me.

"Holy Jesus, you must be a man of God!"

He explained
his dog had a bad reputation
for treating strangers viciously,
especially White men
dressed in blue suits.

I searched for a reason,
momentarily speechless,
guessing the dog knew
somehow

my love for Rudy.
Besides,
I came in singing,
"Fly Me to the Moon,"
something I learned in church
one afternoon when the preacher
was out for his rounds.

An Uncertain Loneliness

I live an uncertain loneliness,
insane again, searching for you,
thinking
I heard you speak my name.
Sometimes I answer
then tumble back,
pretending
you are here again!

I live an uncertain loneliness
between intensities.
Drawn evenly,
bow across the cello,
a resonance
I cannot sustain,
too many rests
between notes.

I live an uncertain loneliness,
friends and lovers
passing through,
some delight, others frighten.
No use pretending
I know what I'm doing
with new faces
who cannot understand
someone
who talks to the dead.

You ask me to come to you.
I don't know how,
though believing
my life is intertwined
in you.
As always,
before I can speak,
you are in my flesh,
everything
within reach, but still …

I live an uncertain loneliness.

Isle of Blue at Kylemore

1

There's an isle of blue
In an ocean of green,
Where the breezes sing with delight.

There's a whispering wave
In the misty haze,
Where seagulls vanish in flight.

With the gentleness
Of twilight's reproach,
The sun sets and disappears.

As the twisting vines,
Melancholy entwines
The silence of all our years.

2

I have searched for redemption
Over these distant waters
For what cannot be spoken or named.

I have sailed on the waves
Of endless days,
Clinging to the bow and the main.

I've drifted, I have swept,
I've run up a debt
To chart a course that was true.

Till I came to this place
Of quiet grace,
In a harbor where I anchored with you.

3

Remember me
For the sweet consolations
That glow in your sacred embrace.

Remember me
For the tender oblations,
Every touch, every time, every place.

And when I reach
Your unbearable light,
All my latent fears will subside.

And I'll lie with you
Forever blue,
With an ocean of green at my side.

CPSIA information can be obtained
at www.ICGtesting.com
Printed in the USA
LVHW010943090121
675850LV00006B/935

9 781480 897816